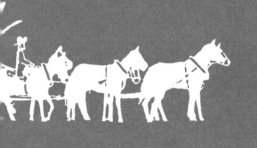

HOW WOULD YOU SURVIVE IN THE
AMERICAN WEST?

Written by
Jacqueline Morley

Illustrated by
David Antram

Created & Designed by
David Salariya

FRANKLIN WATTS
A Division of Grolier Publishing

NEW YORK • LONDON • HONG KONG • SYDNEY
DANBURY, CONNECTICUT

David Salariya   *Director*
Penny Clarke   *Editor*
Dr. John Huitson   *Consultant*

JACQUELINE MORLEY

is a graduate of Somerville College, Oxford. She has taught English and History, and now works as a freelance writer. She has written historical fiction and nonfiction for children and has a particular interest in the history of everyday life. She has also written **Entertainment** and **Clothes** in the Timelines series, **An Egyptian Pyramid** in the Inside Story series, and **How Would You Survive as a Viking?**

DAVID ANTRAM

was born in Brighton in 1958. He studied at Eastbourne College of Art in England and then worked in advertising for fifteen years. He lives in England with his wife and two children.

DAVID SALARIYA

was born in Dundee, Scotland, where he studied illustration and printmaking. He has illustrated a wide range of books on botanical, historical, and mythical subjects. He has created and designed many new series of books for publishers in the United Kingdom and the United States. In 1989 he established the Salariya Book Company. He lives in England with his wife, the illustrator Shirley Willis.

Library of Congress Cataloging-in-Publication Data

Morley, Jacqueline.
    How would you survive in the American West?/by Jacqueline Morley; created and designed by David Salariya.
        p.   cm. — (How would you survive?)
    Includes index.

    ISBN 0-531-14382-1
    1. Frontier and pioneer life — West (U.S.) — Juvenile literature.
    2. Wilderness survival — West (U.S.) — History —19th century — Juvenile literature. 3. West (U.S.) — Social life and customs — Juvenile literature. I. Salariya, David. II. Title. III. Series.
F596.M684 1995
978–dc20
                                        95–17603
                                        CIP AC

Printed in Belgium

First published in the United States in 1995 by Franklin Watts

FRANKLIN WATTS
95 Madison Avenue
New York, NY 10016

DR. JOHN HUITSON

was born in North Shields in 1930. He studied at the University of Durham and then became principal of Darlington College of Education. In 1979 he joined the American Museum in Britain, in Bath, as deputy director and director of education. He retired in 1995.

CONTENTS

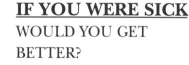

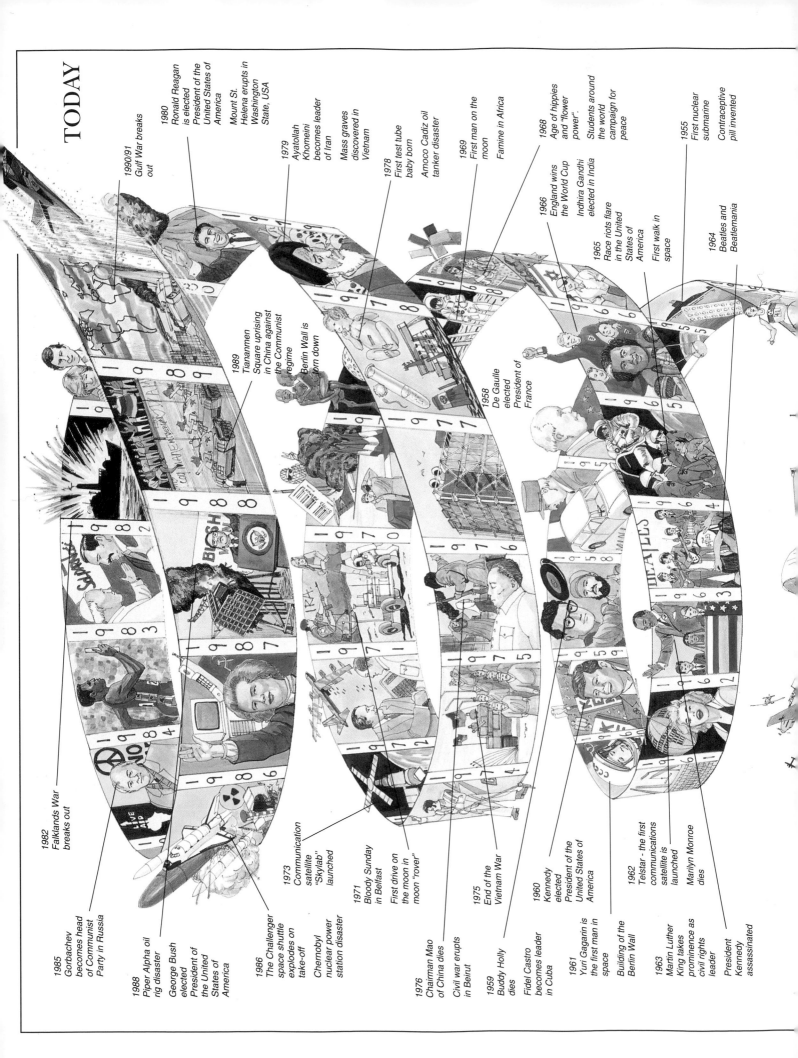

TODAY

1990/91
Gulf War breaks
out

1980
Ronald Reagan
is elected
President of the
United States of
America

Mount St.
Helena erupts in
Washington
State, USA

1979
Ayatollah
Khomeini
becomes leader
of Iran

Mass graves
discovered in
Vietnam

1978
First test tube
baby born

Amoco Cadiz oil
tanker disaster

1969
First man on the
moon

Famine in Africa

1968
Age of hippies
and "flower
power".

Students around
the world
campaign for
peace

1966
England wins
the World Cup

Indhira Gandhi
elected in India

1965
Race riots flare
in the United
States of
America

First walk in
space

1955
First nuclear
submarine

Contraceptive
pill invented

1964
Beatles and
Beatlemania

1989
Tiananmen
Square uprising
in China against
the Communist
regime

Berlin Wall is
born down

1958
De Gaulle
elected
President of
France

1982
Falklands War
breaks out

1985
Gorbachev
becomes head
of Communist
Party in Russia

1988
Piper Alpha oil
rig disaster

George Bush
elected
President of the
United States of
America

1986
The Challenger
space shuttle
explodes on
take-off

Chernobyl
nuclear power
station disaster

1973
Communication
satellite
"Skylab"
launched

1971
Bloody Sunday
in Belfast

First drive on
the moon in
moon "rover"

1975
End of the
Vietnam War

1976
Chairman Mao
of China dies

Civil war erupts
in Beirut

1959
Buddy Holly
dies

Fidel Castro
becomes leader
in Cuba

1960
Kennedy
elected
President of the
United States of
America

1961
Yuri Gagarin is
the first man in
space

Building of the
Berlin Wall

1963
Martin Luther
King takes
prominence as
civil rights
leader

President
Kennedy
assassinated

1962
Telstar - the first
communications
satellite is
launched

Marilyn Monroe
dies

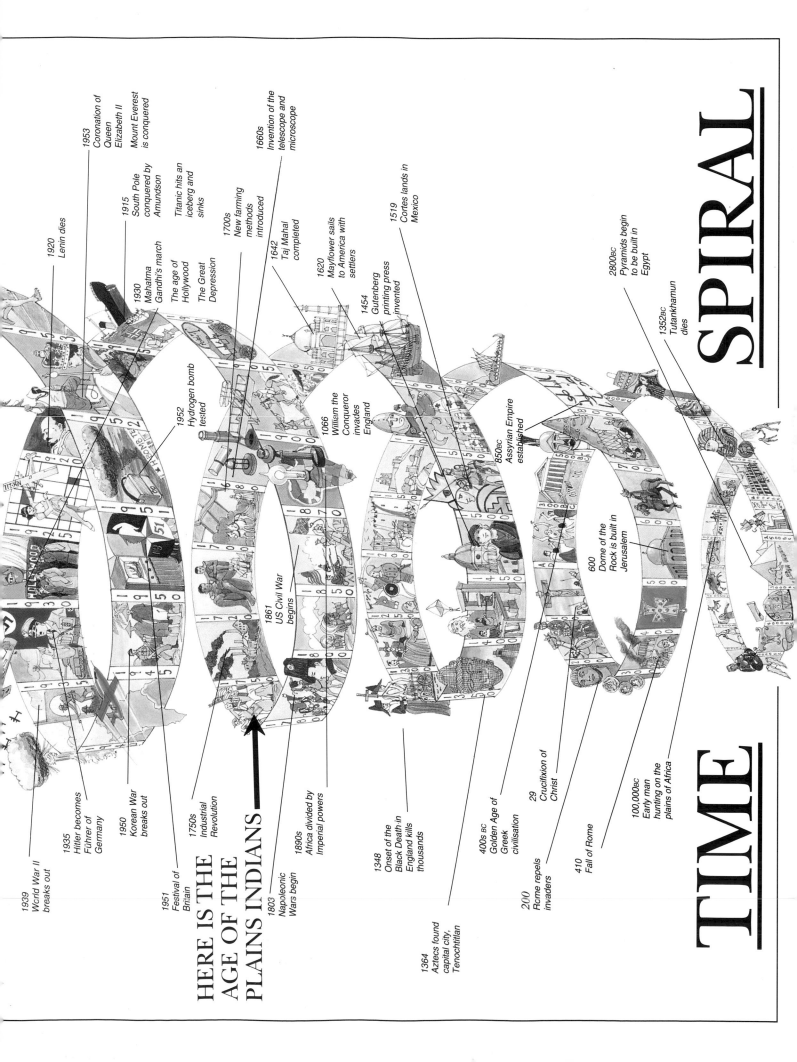

SPIRAL

TIME

HERE IS THE AGE OF THE PLAINS INDIANS

1939 World War II breaks out

1935 Hitler becomes Führer of Germany

1920 Lenin dies

1953 Coronation of Queen Elizabeth II

Mount Everest is conquered

1660s Invention of the telescope and microscope

1915 South Pole conquered by Amundsen

Titanic hits an iceberg and sinks

1700s New farming methods introduced

1642 Taj Mahal completed

1519 Cortes lands in Mexico

1930 Mahatma Gandhi's march

The age of Hollywood

The Great Depression

1620 Mayflower sails to America with settlers

1952 Hydrogen bomb tested

1454 Gutenberg printing press invented

1066 William the Conqueror invades England

850BC Assyrian Empire established

2800BC Pyramids begin to be built in Egypt

1352BC Tutankhamun dies

1950 Korean War breaks out

1951 Festival of Britain

1750s Industrial Revolution

1861 US Civil War begins

600 Dome of the Rock is built in Jerusalem

1803 Napoleonic Wars begin

1890s Africa divided by Imperial powers

1348 Onset of the Black Death in England kills thousands

400s BC Golden Age of Greek civilisation

29 Crucifixion of Christ

100,000BC Early man hunting on the plains of Africa

1364 Aztecs found capital city, Tenochtitlan

200 Rome repels invaders

410 Fall of Rome

A Journey

THIS BOOK takes you on a journey across two-thirds of the vast continent of North America, a distance of over 2,000 miles (3,220 km). Today you could make the trip in four days by road, or in four hours by jet, but you must imagine that you are traveling in the mid-nineteenth century, fifty years before the car appeared. You will be going in an ox-drawn wagon – a five-month trip, at least. If anything happens to your oxen you may have to walk.

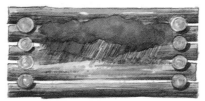

Landscape

WHAT LIES ahead of you? No towns, nothing you would recognize as a village or even a farm. For weeks you cross a vast grassland, extremely hot by day, cold by night, and swept by violent storms; then across the grim, snow-capped Rocky Mountains. Still your journey is only half done. Ahead lies a wilderness just as vast – scrubby desert, canyons, and forests – separating you from your goal, the beckoning land of California or Oregon.

Animals

IN THOSE DAYS, the grassy plains east of the Rockies were home to millions of bison, more commonly called buffalo, in herds so big that the land was sometimes black with them. Elk and antelope roamed the plains. In the forests of the Rockies and in the wilderness beyond lurked black bears and the dangerous grizzly bear. Everywhere there were wolves and scavenging coyotes.

Beaver

LEWIS AND CLARK failed to find an easy way west, but reported on the area's vast mountain forests, teeming with beaver, an animal prized for its fur, which was used for making fashionable hats. The British were making fortunes from it in Canada. This was enough to send adventurous Americans into the wilderness. Fur trappers began to explore the Rocky Mountains. In 1824, or maybe earlier, they found an easy way over, via South Pass.

Mountain Men

TO CATCH ENOUGH beaver to make a living, fur trappers spent most of the year roughing it in the mountains. They learned from the Indians which trails to take and how to survive in the wilderness. These tough mountain men, as they were called, loved life in the wilderness. They never made much money. The big profits were made by the fur companies that bought the furs and exported them.

Traders

SINCE THE 1790s, U.S. ships had been trading along the Pacific, in California and in the "Oregon country" to its north, where British fur traders were in control. The new South Pass route made merchants wonder whether overland trade might not be cheaper and more profitable. In 1832, trader Nathaniel Wyeth took pack mules to Oregon. He was the first to negotiate the route later called the "Oregon Trail."

BASIC FACTS ABOUT LIFE ON THE TRAIL

Indians

THIS LAND WAS NOT empty. The people living there roamed freely in it according to their needs. On the plains lived hunters who followed the herds of buffalo. Farther west, game was scarce and berries and roots were the main food. Nearer the Pacific, people fished the salmon rivers and grew a few crops. European settlers called them all by the name that Columbus had given the native peoples of America: "Indians."

Europeans

EUROPEAN POWERS had fought each other for land in North America since the sixteenth century. By 1800, Spain claimed the area from California to the Rockies, much of it unexplored. The British had Canada. Britain's former east coast colonies, the United States, held the land from the Atlantic to the Mississippi. That left a huge, largely unknown region known as Louisiana in the middle, owned at various times by Spain or France.

Exploration

IN 1803 the French sold this land to the Americans, more than doubling the country's size. In 1804 U.S. President Jefferson sent a team, led by two army officers, Lewis and Clark, to explore this land. They went up the Missouri River, hoping to find a pass over the Rockies and a river flowing west to the coast. With the help of an Indian woman called Sacagawea, they toiled over the Rockies and, after epic hardships, reached the Pacific Ocean.

Missionaries

THE NEXT to go west were missionaries, responding to what they saw as the native people's need for Christianity. One of the first who went to Oregon, in 1834, was so enthusiastic about establishing an American colony there that he returned east to drum up support for the idea. Americans who had sailed to California and stayed to settle had similar ideas. If Americans could get there overland, those regions could be theirs.

Propaganda

DESPITE THE VAST distances to be crossed, the idea of going west soon caught on. Developers were eager to promote it. They wrote to newspapers and spoke at meetings. They described the delights of Oregon or California and the riches awaiting those with the vision to go there. Difficulties were brushed aside. Healthy families, they said, could easily get their wagons over the mountains to this smiling land.

Westward Bound

LET'S SUPPOSE that you have joined one of the first large wagon trains, in 1843 or soon after, when the trail was new and its perils unforeseen. Why wait longer? The first to arrive will get the pick of the land. Stock up your wagon, choose a name for it, and paint it on the wagon. Here are some that went on the trail: *Red Rover, Sweet Sallie, Prairie Bird, Flora, Tornado Train, Never Say Die.* Good luck on the westward trail!

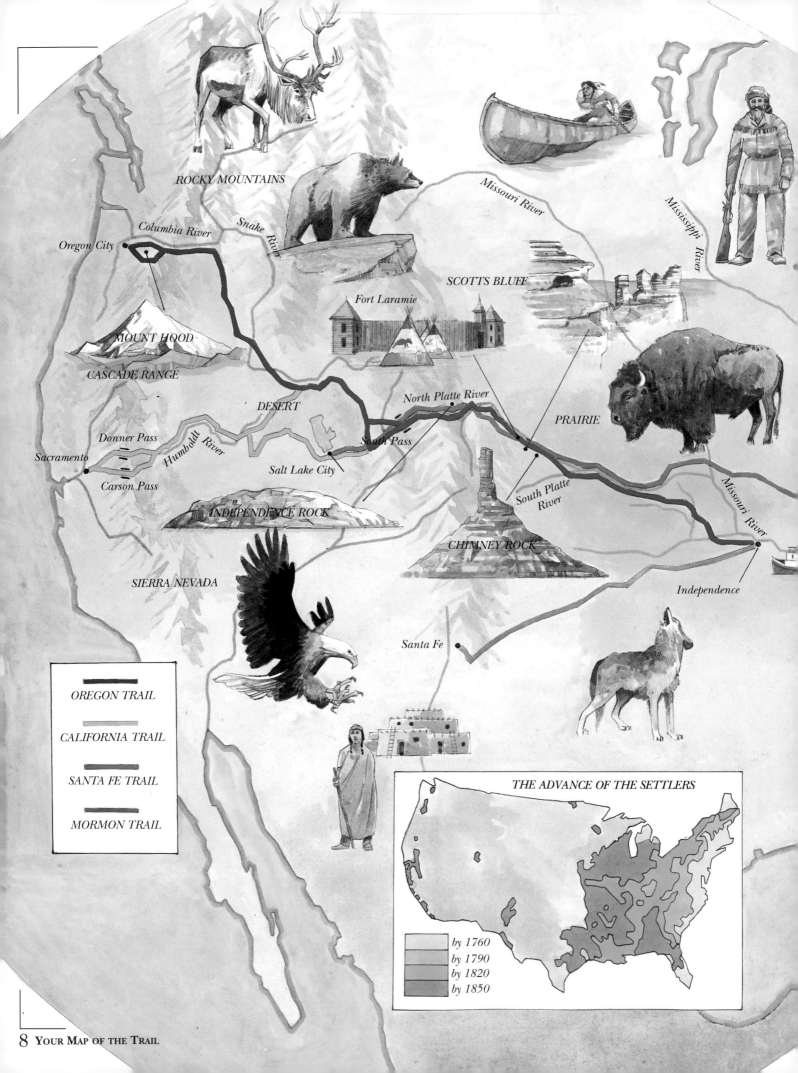

ROCKY MOUNTAINS

Missouri River

Mississippi River

Columbia River

Snake River

Oregon City

SCOTTS BLUFF

Fort Laramie

MOUNT HOOD

CASCADE RANGE

DESERT

North Platte River

PRAIRIE

South Pass

Donner Pass

Humboldt River

Sacramento

Salt Lake City

South Platte River

Carson Pass

INDEPENDENCE ROCK

Missouri River

CHIMNEY ROCK

SIERRA NEVADA

Independence

Santa Fe

━━━ OREGON TRAIL

━━━ CALIFORNIA TRAIL

━━━ SANTA FE TRAIL

━━━ MORMON TRAIL

THE ADVANCE OF THE SETTLERS

by 1760
by 1790
by 1820
by 1850

YOUR MAP OF THE TRAIL

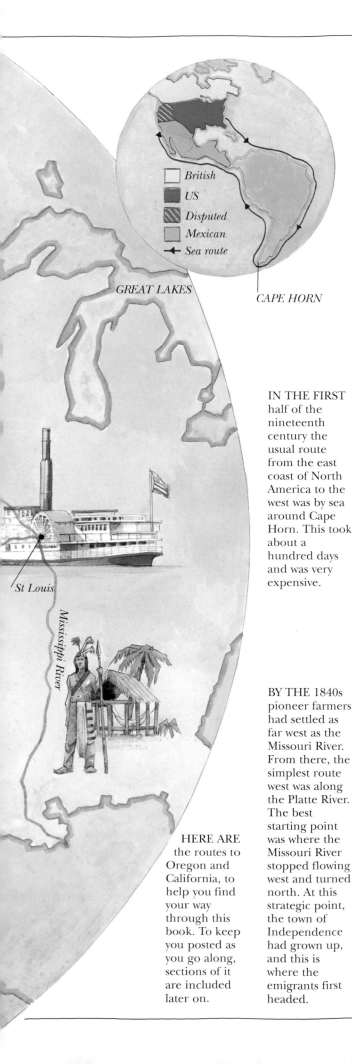

GREAT LAKES

CAPE HORN

St Louis

Mississippi River

YOU MAY WONDER why the settlers who went to California and Oregon in the 1840s should have gone so far. What was wrong with the land in between? Lots of people live there today. But pioneer Americans were looking for good farmland. They believed that good soil always grew good trees. They had no use for the plains that stretched monotonously to the Rocky Mountains. In their opinion, the Indians were welcome to them. On maps, this huge area was labeled "the Great American Desert." And what little they knew of the lands just beyond the Rockies made them certain those were even worse.

The far west, by contrast, sounded full of hope. If the American people could get there overland, America could claim it. That appealed to the settlers' patriotic spirit, for Mexico held California and the British were in Oregon. This is why the settlers were called emigrants. Those who went west before 1847 were leaving the United States, perhaps for good.

British

US

Disputed

Mexican

← **Sea route**

IN THE FIRST half of the nineteenth century the usual route from the east coast of North America to the west was by sea around Cape Horn. This took about a hundred days and was very expensive.

BY THE 1840s pioneer farmers had settled as far west as the Missouri River. From there, the simplest route west was along the Platte River. The best starting point was where the Missouri River stopped flowing west and turned north. At this strategic point, the town of Independence had grown up, and this is where the emigrants first headed.

HERE ARE the routes to Oregon and California, to help you find your way through this book. To keep you posted as you go along, sections of it are included later on.

ARRIVAL IN "UTOPIA." Oregon promoters described it as the loveliest country on earth, where, according to one prospectus, "vegetables, grain, and cattle will require comparatively little labor." A family of settlers arrive fit and smiling, and gaze from their trim wagon upon a happy scene. But it existed only in their imagination and the promoters' advertisements.

BEGIN YOUR NEW LIFE HERE

WHERE IS this town? Why is it so crowded, and what is everyone doing? *Go to pages 14-15*

HERE AND ON the next two pages is a panorama of the westward trail. It is not meant to be a true-to-life picture of the pioneers' routes, for you would not have found all these activities and varied scenery so close together. It is your guide to this book. Start wherever you wish and follow the Q options.

WHY ARE these wagons arranged in a circle? *Go to pages 18-19*

ARE THESE Indians likely to be friendly? *Go to pages 24-25 and 40*

WHAT ARE people putting into their wagons? *Go to pages 16-17*

WHAT IS this huge herd of animals? Are they dangerous? Could they be useful?
Go to page 21

THIS IS a fort, which the wagoners pass on their way. Why was it built out in the wilderness? What goes on inside? Will the pioneers get help there?
Go to pages 28-29

THESE WAGONERS have just set off and are having a race. Why are they doing that? Is it a good idea? *Go to pages 17 and 18-19*

WHAT ARE these children collecting?
Go to page 22

WHY ARE these men putting up a flag by the river?
Go to page 18

THESE PEOPLE no longer have animals to pull their wagon. What could have happened to them, and what can their owners do now?
Go to page 27

THE PIONEERS often have to cross wide rivers. There are no bridges. How will the wagon train get across?
Go to page 26

THIS WAGON has lost a wheel, and one of its oxen is lame. Why did such things happen so often, and what could be done about them?
Go to page 20

WHAT IS this man writing? *Go to pages 42-43*

THIS WOMAN is washing her family's clothes in a stream. How did women cope with life on the trail? *Go to pages 22-23*

WHO LEFT this message nailed to a stick? What might it say? *Go to pages 30-31*

WHAT SORT of weather did the travelers face? *Go to pages 20 and 37*

THE MEMBERS of this train are arguing over whether to take a shortcut. Did this really shorten the journey time? *Go to page 37*

WHAT are these men carrying? Where are they going and why? *Go to page 33*

HOW DID the
wagons cross
the Rocky
Mountains?
Go to page 32

HOW DID
people cope
with the last
stretch of the
journey?
Go to pages 36-37

THIS FAMILY is
cutting down
trees to build a
house on their
new land in the
West. How did
they set up
housekeeping?
Go to pages 38-39

THESE
PEOPLE have
been delayed
and are still in
the mountains
when winter
comes. Are they
likely to get
through?
Go to page 37

THIS OX was
thirsty, but after
it drank it
became really
ill. What has
happened?
Go to page 22

WHY ARE
these people
chopping up
their wagon?
Go to page 36

THIS MAN is
feeling very ill.
Will he die?
Go to pages 34-35

SOMEONE
has been shot
dead. Could this
be murder?
Go to pages 26-27

A person promoting settlement of the West comes to town. He tells of wonderful opportunities out West.

Life is hard for you, and farming profits are down. You sell your farm to buy equipment for the move west.

As soon as spring approaches, you must set off. It is very hard to say good-bye to parents you may never see again

Your newly painted wagon, with a tough canvas cover to keep out sun and rain, sets off cross-country to Independence.

Q

You have suddenly gotten a very painful toothache. Can you get help?
Go to page 35

THE MEETING POINT
WHERE WOULD YOUR JOURNEY BEGIN?

I T IS A SPRING DAY in the early 1840s. The town of Independence, Missouri, is packed to bursting. Its storekeepers are happy with the tumult; for years the wagon trains that take goods south to sell at Santa Fe have started out from here, and fitting out wagons is its speciality. Now westbound wagons fill the town as well.

The best way to reach Independence was by steamboat from St. Louis. This could take six or seven days as the boat fought with the current and sandbars of the Missouri River.

The main street of Independence is packed with people buying supplies. Some are making final purchases, but those who have come from afar get most things here.

Some well-off farmers arrive with big herds of cattle, which they plan to take west as an investment. They have heard that cattle bring high prices there. The herds of cattle cavort and bellow out of control. They will be a nuisance on the trip.

Pioneers gathered at Independence and waited for enough wagons to arrive to form a "train." There was safety in numbers when unknown dangers might lie in wait ahead.

Anxious pioneers asked the advice of everyone in town. Rumors flew about: this year the grass was very late; the streams were swollen with the rain; the streams were low and water would be scarce; the Indians had attacked a previous train; the Indians did not attack at all.

The best advice came from mountain men: never risk being short of the essentials of firewood, water, and grass for your animals. Do not start too soon or the grass will be too short to keep your animals fed; do not start too late or you will not get over the mountains before they are blocked by snow.

ARRIVING BY BOAT

The boat from St. Louis will be crowded. If you can't get a cabin, you will have to sleep where you can.

These missionary couples are Oregon-bound to preach Christianity to the Indians. Most pioneers were more like the tough Missouri family below. They are pioneer farmers on the westernmost fringe of the settled states. They are seeking a still emptier land where they can live exactly as they choose.

The boat gets stuck on a "snag." You fume at the delay. The friends you're joining may leave without you.

You discover the landing stage is some miles from the town. You haggle to hire some horses to get you there.

There is nonstop hammering and banging from the blacksmiths' sheds, where wagons are being repaired and horses, mules, and oxen shod. The way is blocked as carts pull up to load; horse dealers push through with strings of animals; mountain men dressed in buckskins give inexperienced travelers advice; stray cattle cause the dogs to bark; and lost children wail.

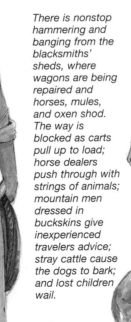

You have no wagon or tent yet. You need a bed for the night, but every inn is full. Perhaps a family will let you sleep under its wagon.

Q

The ideal spot for your new house has a tree in the way. It is too big to chop with an ax. What can you do?
Go to page 39

About forty families are camped beyond the town – enough now to set off.

A young man with no money hangs around, hoping to be hired as extra help on the trip.

If he expects an easy ride he is mistaken. He will have to work hard.

STOCKING UP
WHAT WOULD YOU NEED FOR THE JOURNEY?

PIONEERS NEEDED WAGONS strong enough to carry people and provisions for five months or more. They had to be made of seasoned hardwood to withstand the trip's extremes of hot, cold, wet, and dry. A large wagon, fully loaded, needed at least three pairs of oxen to draw it.

Deciding what went in the wagon was crucial. Weight was very important. You had to take food for many weeks – to run out meant disaster – you needed tents, tools, guns, bedding, clothes, cooking equipment, soap, and candles. What about the medicine chest, some books, Mother's rocking chair, the old grandfather clock? Before adding those, remember that the wagon and everything in it will be useless if the weight wears out the oxen.

The ideal solution was to take more than one wagon, and many families did. A family of four could manage with a single wagon, although they would be uncomfortable, as stores would take most of the space.

Draft animals worked in teams made up of several pairs. Mules wore collars; oxen wore a yoke.

Ox yoke

Some people took a "walking larder" – a few sheep and cattle to be killed and eaten on the way.

Large sacks held beans, flour, rice, cornmeal, and dried peaches and apples. Bacon was put in barrels packed with bran, so that hot sun would not melt the fat.

Each man took a rifle or shotgun and put a pistol or bowie knife in his belt.

Farm tools and carpentry tools would be the first things needed on arrival, to make the new home and grow food. The plow and long-handled tools were strapped to the wagon's sides.

Would it be better to buy mules or oxen to pull your wagon? There are lots of people to give advice.

Mules go faster, but can be tricky. They hold their breath as straps are tightened, then let it out so the load slips.

This mule is playing a typical trick. It keeps its legs rigid and no matter how hard its owner tugs, it will not move.

Mules know when they have an inexperienced driver and will bolt. One wagon hits a tree. Another heads for the river.

Bucket of grease

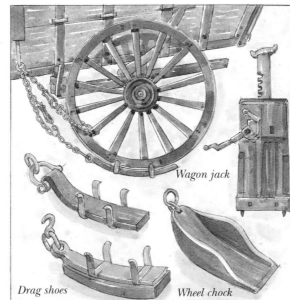

On steep slopes, wheels were locked with a chain, to stop the wagon from rolling onto the team. Drag shoes stopped rims from wearing flat when wheels locked. To replace a wheel use a jack to support the wagon.

Wagon jack

Drag shoes

Wheel chock

Q

What will you eat when the bacon runs out?
Go to pages 22-23

You may be homesick, especially if your husband decided on the move. You did your duty as a wife, but you keep thinking of your parents. You mail them a letter saying everything is fine.

How will you find the way? You could follow the trail made by the fur traders, but it may disappear. You need a guide. Luckily, mountain men are waiting to be hired.

Pioneers are tough-minded people. Arguments soon break out. Who gives the orders? Everyone agrees the train needs a captain. The worst quarrels are over who should be the captain.

Mule collars

Food and drink for a family of four:
flour 600lb (272kg)
biscuits 120lb (54kg)
bacon 400lb (181kg)
coffee 60lb (27kg)
tea 4lb (2kg)
sugar 100lb (45kg)
lard 200lb (91 kg)

beans 200lb (91kg)
dried fruit 120lb (54kg)
salt 40lb (18kg)
pepper 8lb (4kg)
baking soda 8lb (4kg)
whiskey 1 keg (about 30 gallons or 136l)

OXEN

Oxen are reliable. They are tougher than mules and will eat poor greenery. If you are starving, they are better meat.

But oxen are slow. You could often be behind another wagon, getting the dust its wheels raise in dry weather.

Oxen are strong. They can haul a wagon up a ravine or drag it out of a mudhole much more easily than mules.

If a shady dealer has sold you an animal that has not been properly broken in, you will find that even oxen can be tricky at times.

Pioneers hold meetings and draw up regulations, but on the day of departure everything is in confusion. No one is in overall control. Teams race to get the best position in the line.

There are quarrels over when to halt for a rest, how long it should be, and what makes a good campsite. But brawling brings its own punishment. You can't drive your team with a black eye.

The men decide to elect officers. Candidates for election run out onto the prairie. Each voter (men only) runs behind the man of his choice. Those with the longest "tails" are elected.

Q
Are you likely to meet hostile Indians?
Go to pages 24-25

SETTING OFF

HOW WOULD THE JOURNEY START?

EVERYONE FEELS in a holiday mood as the wagons bump over the sunny prairie – nothing but lush waving grass, stretching as far as the eye can see. The teams plod along at about two miles (3.2km) an hour. Going faster would only wear them out.

They do about twenty miles (32km) on a good day. Fifteen miles (24km) was average.

A Day's Routine

4:00 A.M. The guards fire rifles to wake the camp. People stretch. The ground or wagon floor is a hard bed.

5:00 A.M. Men ride off to round up the cattle. They are allowed to graze at night outside the corral to get good grass.

5:30 A.M. The women have got the children up and breakfast is ready. Bacon and corn porridge are popular.

6:30 A.M. While the women rinse the tin plates and mugs in the river and stow the bedding, the men take down tents and reload them in the wagons.

The first lap is over rolling grassland, crossed by wooded streams, to the Platte River, then westward along its south bank.

The father of each family drove the wagon, unless he had hired a teamster and was free to ride alongside.

The wagon train straggled in a long line across the prairie. Mule-drawn wagons, which were the speediest, led the way. Then came those with ox teams. Loose horses and mules were driven along behind. Last came the slow, snorting herd of cattle.

Q

Will all the trip be such a pleasant ride?
Go to pages 36-37

6:50 A.M. Each family assembles its team and hitches them to the wagons.

7:00 A.M. A trumpeter signals the start. Each wagon moves up a place daily.

7:30 A.M. Men ride carrying shovels. They will dig out a path if necessary.

10:00 A.M. At a river, they find the best place for fording and raise a flag.

Midday. "Nooning time." Pioneers and animals take a welcome break, to eat and drink.

1:00 P.M. The officers judge between a wagoner and his hired man.

At first, people dreaded that Indians might attack. At night, the wagons were closely parked and linked by ox chains to make an enclosure known as a corral. In fact, they soon realized that the Indians were most unlikely to attack. The corral's main use was to keep valuable animals out of their reach.

Keeping watch is unpopular, but it is the only way to stop the Pawnee Indians from taking the animals.

Sitting up alone, listening in the dark, makes you jumpy. One man shot a mule, thinking it was an Indian in disguise.

After a long day, you find you just can't keep your eyes open. But no one will know if you take a little nap.

The next guard found you fast asleep! As a punishment the court says you must walk for a whole day, leading your horse.

After a week or so, the long daily routine begins to make tempers fray. Strong-minded farmers do not like being told what to do. They argue over where to camp, whether to take a rest day, and who should do guard duty. Pioneers without extra animals do not see why they should take a turn on guard, just to stop other people's animals from being stolen by the Indians. And cattle slow the whole train, anyway! These impatient people soon form a group that presses ahead, leaving the cattle owners to follow in a slow-moving "cow column." Disagreements often split up trains. If it happens to yours, stay with the party with the most experienced guide.

Women and children were expected to ride in the wagons, but this gave them such a jolting that they were glad to get out and walk as much as possible through the flowery grass.

3:00 P.M. A driver nods off. His oxen stop. The train goes on. He will catch up later.

5:00 P.M. A good campsite has been found. Each wagon is directed to form the corral.

6:00 P.M. Smoke rises from campfires as families unpack and make supper.

7:00 P.M. Young people dance. Men smoke and chat. Mothers still have chores to do.

8:00 P.M. As the guard comes on duty. The night noises of the prairie begin.

Midnight. A new guard comes on duty. "Nothing to report," he is told. Wolves' eyes gleam.

Q

How did women spend the day? What work did they do?
Go to pages 22-23

Many oxen have cracked and bleeding hooves. One of them steps on a prickly pear.

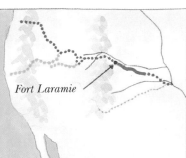

Fort Laramie

The Platte River is wide and too shallow for boats, but it provides pioneers with water as they follow it for 300 miles (480km) towards the Rockies.

STORMS AND DUST
HOW WOULD YOU COPE?

THE WEATHER is often more of an enemy than the Indians. Clouds pile up suddenly and burst in violent storms. Black skies flare with lightning, and thunder seems to shake the prairie.

As the route climbs higher the plain grows parched and sandy, with not a tree in sight. The June sun is blistering; the nights are frosty. A west wind whips the sandy soil into clouds of stinging dust and drives it in the travelers' faces. Their eyes smart; their lips puff and split.

Its hoof soon becomes swollen and starts to fester. Wash the infected area thoroughly with strong soap.

Scrape away the diseased flesh with a knife and sterilize the wound by pouring on boiling pitch, or tar.

Make a protective moccasin from buffalo hide, turned raw side out, and tie it on securely. The other feet may need them, too.

The oxen are now gaunt and weary. They heave the wagons across deep ruts that buffalo have worn in the ground as they go down to the river. As a wheel jolted over one of these, its axle might snap.

Q

Would it be a good idea to take a shortcut?
Go to page 37

Go to page 37

Wind tears off the wagon covers. Lightning makes teams rear and cattle stampede. The rain blots out everything. In minutes, people are drenched, campsites become seas of mud, tents are blown away, bedding soaked.

Not again! Another wheel has shed its tire. The intense dry heat is making all the wagon timbers warp and shrink. As the wooden rims contract, the metal tires get loose and fall off.

You will have to enlarge the wheel rim. You do this by adding wood. Carve small pieces of wood into curves and nail them around the outer rim. Then heat the tire.

Slip the hot tire over the wheel. It will go on because the heat expanded the metal. Then throw a bucket of water over the wheel. This will make the metal contract, so the tire fits tightly.

The Plains Indians relied entirely on the buffalo for their needs. It provided their meat. They made its skin into clothes, shoes, ropes, tents, and boats, its bones into tools and ceremonial objects, and its sinews into thread. They moved their camps to follow the herds over the plains.

Impressed wagoners look on as a galloping Indian kills a buffalo with a single arrow.

Prairie dogs dived into their burrows with little yelps of alarm as the wagon train went by.

LOST ON THE PLAINS

You have gone shooting. Buffalo are not easy to kill. Unless you hit them in the right spot, they just lumber away.

You keep chasing a particular animal and find you are lost. Whichever way you look, you see nothing but grass.

Which is the way to the river? You have no idea. Your horse stumbles in a prairie dog's hole and is lamed.

Leading it aimlessly, you notice a path worn through the grass. A buffalo track! These always lead down to the river. You are no longer lost.

Q

If your wagon is flooded or your oxen are lost, will any one help?
Go to pages 30-31

BUFFALO

DO YOU FEAR THEM?

THE PLAINS that lined the upper Platte River were the home of huge herds of buffalo. They lumbered down in long lines, single file, to the river to drink. Whenever a wagon train sighted them, the men seized their guns and galloped off on a hunting spree, shooting every buffalo they could. They gave no thought to what the Indians felt about this.

Wagoners hear a rumbling like thunder and see a dark mass pouring down a hill toward them. The train is in the path of stampeding buffalo. There is no hope that the beasts will stop.

A stampede appearing suddenly over the edge of the plateau can take an encampment by surprise. There is no time to move the wagons. Men set fire to the prairie, hoping to turn the herd.

Stampeding buffalo can bring out the wild streak in your own beasts and set them bolting till they are exhausted. Cattle break legs; wheels splinter; people are run over.

WOMEN'S WORK

HOW WOULD YOU SPEND YOUR TIME?

Good drinking water is vital. Buffalo churn up the water as they cross the Platte River so it is undrinkable.

The Platte River is full of sand anyway. You may find clearer water by digging a well nearby.

Near the Rockies many springs and pools are alkaline. People become ill and cattle may die from drinking such water.

This boy says his drink is full of little "wigglers"! His mother tells him to be glad: the water can't be poisonous if they can live in it.

Q

Have any of the pioneers' diaries survived?
Go to pages 42-43

MOST PIONEER FAMILIES were tough farmers, used to a life where everyone worked hard, but men did one type of work and women another. Men ran the farm, women did the housekeeping. On the trail, it was the same. Men made the decisions, drove the teams, and did the hunting. Women packed, unpacked, cooked, washed, and mended.

If people were really hungry, they ate a whole buffalo. More often, they took only the best bits – the tongue and hump ribs.

A family cooking buffalo steaks. They have hung strips of meat to dry as well. The movements of the buffalo are unpredictable; you may not see them again, so it is wise to dry meat for future use.

A WOMAN'S DAY

You wake with a queasy feeling, hoping it isn't dysentery, get the children up and make breakfast.

You start to repack and find that a pile of clothes fell off the wagon last night; an ox has eaten your dress.

Walking is a change from the wagon. You can have a talk, but you have to carry the toddler.

At the noon break, the drivers and animals rest awhile. You go collecting buffalo chips for tonight.

Today, the women have insisted on making a longer stop to wash a few clothes in the river.

You spread them on the bank to dry but the wind covers them with sand, and they are no cleaner.

MAKING BREAD:
Mix flour, water, salt, and baking soda in a basin.

Try to keep out the sand, and then roll it flat. Cook it for two hours, with hot buffalo chips on the pan lid. If it rains, keep an umbrella over it.

Buffalo

After weeks of bacon only, fresh buffalo is a treat.

Elk or pronghorn (which they called antelope) were also good. Or try a prairie dog!

The rain has got in and soaked your stores. The coffee is damp, the sugar is liquid, the flour is full of lumps.

You open a sack to check the bacon. It has a very odd smell. It has gone bad and is full of maggots.

Elk

Prairie dog

Some dogs of the Indians' have been chewing your bag of dried buffalo. It's too precious to waste, so you use it.

Cooking was a backbreaking job. Everything had to be prepared on the ground, as there were no tables. Some women tried to keep up civilized standards by using rubber tablecloths and putting out boxes as seats. All water had to be carried from the river. One tired woman washed up in leftover tea.

On the high plateau, there was not a stick of wood to light a fire, so people used "buffalo chips" (dry buffalo dung), which were burned in a trench cut in the turf. The chips glowed with a tiny flame, enough to cook over, but not much comfort on a cold night. Iron pans were put on the fire, or pots were hung over it on a contraption of poles. If the poles collapsed, everyone got ashes in their food.

Pronghorn

You've had no meat for two weeks. Not a buffalo in sight. You find a dying ox abandoned by its owners and kill that. Meat at last!

You try to bathe but have to flee from swarms of mosquitoes. Every inch of you is bitten.

You spend the afternoon being shaken up in the wagon, caring for a baby whose mother is ill.

The evening meal. There is no fresh meat so you boil together flour and strips of dried buffalo.

After supper you make up beds in the tent and tuck in your baby. Then you give his sister her lessons.

There is still mending to do, tomorrow's lunch to get, stores to check, and the wagon to organize.

Nearly bedtime, but the men are still talking. There is just time to write about the day in your diary.

Q

You want to leave a message for friends traveling in another wagon train. How can you do that?
Go to page 31

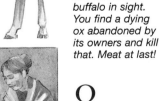

Indians are often willing to trade. They will swap buffalo robes and moccasins for knives, clothes, mirrors, or beads.

Indians saved the lives of many pioneers by telling them where to find water in the desert.

This Paiute chief is accompanying a band of lost pioneers, in case they have not understood his directions.

If your food runs out and there is no game, you have to eat wild plants or starve. Local Indians will show you which plants are safe to eat.

Q

What happened when the Indians turned against the white man?
Go to page 40

a Blackfeet of the north plains.
b Paiute of the plateau beyond the Rockies.
c Sioux of the central plains.
d Pawnee of the eastern plains
e Crow, the Siouxs' traditional enemy.
f Mandan, from the upper Missouri. By the 1840s, most had died of white people's diseases.

INDIANS
HOW WOULD YOU FEEL ABOUT THEM?

PIONEERS BEGAN their journey full of fears about the Indians. Most pioneers knew almost nothing about the Indians who lived in the lands they would be traveling through. Many did not even know that there were many separate Indian nations with different languages and ways of life. The tribes of the plains were buffalo hunters; those west of the Rockies gathered seeds and hunted small animals; in the far south they were farmers; in the northwest they were salmon fishers, hunters, and gatherers.

If you visit a tribe to trade, its chief will welcome you, once he is satisfied that you mean no harm. A meal will be cooked and you will be expected to smoke the pipe of peace.

Indians can explain the route ahead and warn you of dry stretches and hostile tribes. They will make a map, drawing rivers in the sand and putting stones for mountains.

Friendly Indians can help in difficult situations. They will pilot wagons over swollen rivers, ferry baggage in their canoes, and swim pioneers' cattle to safety.

An Indian chief flings down his spear to warn a pioneer train that it is entering his people's territory and must pay for the right to cross it. The U.S. government recognized the Indians' right to charge a toll in return for guaranteeing pioneers' safety. If trains refused to pay, Indians did not see why they should keep their side of the bargain.

You will not get the better of an Indian in a bargain over a horse. They will not sell a good one.

Indians who offer to "find" stolen animals may be the thieves, expecting a reward.

Early pioneers complained that Indians stole whatever they could, but otherwise they found them friendly and helpful. There was no serious trouble until after 1849, when impatient trigger-happy people swarmed onto the trail, mistreating Indians and recklessly shooting buffalo. Yet, between 1840 and 1860, Indians killed fewer than 370 pioneers while pioneers killed about 425 Indians.

When a wagon train used a ferry run by Pawnees and then refused to pay, the Pawnees plundered it.

Never wander off on your own, thinking you'll catch up later. It's asking for trouble. This man stopped to sketch and Indians took everything he had!

A family watches with alarm and curiosity as Plains Indians ride past. The first meeting with Indians was an exciting moment.

The Indians are moving in search of buffalo. They have no fixed home, but set up their tepees wherever the hunting is good.

This Indian brought his own oxen to help a pioneer whose animals were too weak to pull a wagon up a steep bank. Indians were often hired as guides and interpreters.

Many Indians showed sympathy for pioneers' hardships. While the father of a family was fording his wagon, an Indian made a fire for his wife and child.

Two Shoshone braves rescued a drowning pioneer whose wagon had capsized in the rapid currents of the Snake River. They were rewarded with clothing and provisions.

Q

Some Indians are married to whites. Where would you find them?
Go to pages 28-29

DISASTER STRIKES
WOULD YOU BE FRIGHTENED?

Never under-estimate the perils of river crossings. Even large rafts can capsize suddenly.

Don't cross unless you have to. A man who took his animals to better grass on the far bank was drowned.

Beware of animals in a panic. They are a hazard on land and much worse on water.

Know what you're doing. A wagoner with too much drink inside him mistook a river for a marsh. He drove in and was never seen again.

D ANGER WAS never far away, but not where pioneers most feared it. More people died in accidents than were killed by Indians. The most common were drownings in the many rivers that had to be crossed. Ninety people drowned in 1850 alone.

By the 1850s there were ferries at many crossings, but hard up travelers still tried to get themselves across and save the ferry charge, often with disastrous results. They might escape with their lives, only to watch helplessly as wagon, provisions, and belongings were swept away.

A wagon overturns in rapid water and is swept downriver. When currents were dangerous, the wagons were linked by chains, to hold them in line, but if a wagon rolled down a bank, or its team floundered in a pothole, the chain took the full weight of the wagon and might give way.

Men rode alongside to guide the teams and try to prevent such disasters.

Q
Which is the most dangerous river of all?
Go to page 36

If a ford is deep, raise the wagon chassis by driving wedges between it and the frame.

If the river is too deep to ford, hollow out logs and make a raft.

If there are no trees for a raft, cover the wagon box in buffalo skins and float it .

Families and baggage go over in Indian-style bullboats. Set a ring of willow branches in the ground, tie the ends together, and lace canes through this framework. Then cover the frame with hide, dry it over a fire, and make it watertight by rubbing in buffalo fat, mixed with ashes.

The nightmare every family dreads: the heat, the dust, the ceaseless work, have brought the patient oxen to their knees.

Without rest and good grass there is no hope of saving them.

Firearms were the next most common cause of fatal accidents. Wagon trains bristled with so many guns that the chances of one going off accidentally, or hitting the wrong target, were extremely high. People killed or maimed themselves as well as other pioneers.

Over the years, there were countless mishaps. People got crushed by moving wagon wheels, or by draft animals. They were thrown by horses, crushed in stampedes, burned in grassfires, and injured in hailstorms. At least six were killed by lightning; four were crushed to death by a falling oak; one even got rabies from a wolf bite. Another dread fate was to lose draft animals. It could mean the difference between life and death.

FATAL ACCIDENTS

Never pull your rifle out of the wagon muzzle first. If the trigger catches in something, you could be shot.

Look out for trailing wagon ropes. You could be dragged along and even killed, if your foot gets entangled in one.

Riding accidents cause many broken bones and deaths. And look out on the ground: a kick in the chest can be fatal.

Small children need watching. A boy who tried to drive while his father was asleep got run over when he fell from the wagon front.

If you do not watch out, your horses and mules will be taken in the night. Plains Indians seldom take oxen, but there are tribes beyond the Rockies so short of food that they will kill them.

Plains Indians are amazingly skillful horse thieves. They can untether the animals without a sound. A man slept with his horse tied to his arm at night, but one morning it was gone.

If you are lucky, you may be able to trace your stolen animals by questioning Indians in the area. They may be hostile to the thieves. But you may search for days, losing precious time.

If your draft animals are stolen and no one has any to lend, your plight is desperate. The train will only wait a day or so. It can't afford to wait longer. It will move on, leaving you behind.

All you can do is to camp beside the trail until another train passes. Someone may have animals you can borrow or buy. Even a pair of cows might get your wagon to the nearest fort.

Maybe no one can help. Then you have to abandon the wagon and walk. But which way? Back east is much shorter, but you aren't going to give up. You plod on to the fort.

Q

What happens at a fort? How many might you pass on your way? Who goes there and why?
Go to pages 28-29

AT THE FORT
WHAT WILL YOU DO?

The head of the fort gives you news about the route ahead – the state of the grass and the attitude of the Indians.

You can buy food at the fort stores, but don't expect the storekeeper's prices to be reasonable. You are at his mercy!

In 1849, Fort Laramie would not buy surplus food from over-loaded gold rushers, so it had to be dumped.

In reaction, next year's trains took far too little. Ugly scenes arose when forts ran out of surplus goods and would not sell to starving people.

Q

What furs would the mountain men bring in?
Go to pages 6-7

AFTER TWO MONTHS' TRAVEL across seemingly endless prairie and plain, you come to a solitary building with palisaded walls and watchtowers, overlooking the Platte River. This is Fort Laramie, a trading station owned by the American Fur Company. The trade is now mainly in buffalo skins. Indians bring dressed skins to the fort in exchange for goods, made by the whites, which company agents bring out from the East.

For the pioneers, the fort is a godsend. Just when their food is running out, their wagons falling apart, their animals at their last gasp, they can rest for a day or two in what seems to their aching bones the lap of luxury.

This odd sight is an ox being reshod. Oxen cannot lift a hoof for shoeing, as horses can. At the fort you put the ox on its back in a trench while you attend to its sore feet.

Now you can give the wagons a thorough overhaul. If a wagon is beyond repair, you can break it up and use the good parts to mend another. But if it's your only wagon you patch it up somehow!

At last the women can give clothes and blankets a thorough washing, instead of rinsing out a few things. You need the whole day, at least, for a proper washday.

Inside the fort: Mothers look on as one of their train argues with the storekeeper; a U.S. soldier on patrol is about to leave; a trader has come in with the convoy of fresh supplies. Squaws snatch up their children and chase their chickens out of the way. They are the wives of company employees who live in the fort. Mountain men have brought in a few furs and are loafing around, hoping for work.

a Fort Walla Walla, a Hudson's Bay Company fort.

b Fort Laramie

c Fort Boise and *d* Fort Hall, both Hudson's Bay Company forts.

e Fort Bridger, a private venture later rebuilt as a U.S. army fort.

The train passes five or six forts along the trail, some owned by fur companies, some by mountain men turned traders. Pioneers find comfort in thinking of their journey not as one huge distance but as treks from fort to fort.

FORT EVENTS

Fort stopovers were a chance to see new faces and have some homemade entertainment.

In 1845, U.S. army officers called Sioux chiefs to a council at Fort Laramie to ensure pioneers' safety.

Afterward, a party of pioneers gave the Sioux a feast beneath the cottonwood trees by the fort.

In 1849, the U.S. government bought Fort Laramie and the Army took it over to give military aid to passing trains and to patrol the trail.

Q
If you want to avoid being seriously ill, buy vegetables at the fort. Why?
Go to pages 34-35

Your draft animals are worn out and thin from lack of good grazing. If you can afford it, trade them in for fresh ones. Yours will be rested and fattened at the fort, and sold to later pioneers.

There's a blacksmith at Fort Laramie. If the smith is not busy you might be able to gather together with other pioneers and hire the smithy for a day. Shoeing is easier with a forge.

You may have to say good-bye to your fur-trapper guide, if he has business here and wants to stay. But there will be others at the fort waiting to be hired.

A HELPING HAND

HOW WOULD YOU HELP?

Pioneers with special skills – carpenters, black-smiths, doctors – are very willing to give help to people in trouble.

If you meet someone riding east, you can send news back home. He will mail your letter at Independence.

A woman is too ill to stand the wagon's jolting. Kindhearted pioneers stop until she can go on.

Trains pool manpower for big tasks, like making a ferry or digging out the banks of a stream, so that wagons can get down to ford it.

Q

Who were the gold rushers? Would you have enjoyed traveling with them?
Go to page 33

HOW WILL YOU get along with other people on the trip? Will they help if you are in trouble? Families certainly had plenty of time to get to know each other and to form dislikes. When each wagon owner could have a different opinion about what the train should be doing, life was never easy. Men became aggressive and used their fists. But the strains of the journey brought out the best in people, too. Quarrels were more than outweighed by kindness. People loaned animals, shared food with those who had run out, welcomed lost strangers from other trains, looked after sick and injured comrades, and helped when wagons broke down. Trains joined forces to cross rivers, hunt for stolen animals, and round up stampeded stock.

140 miles to Sacramento you ar a Damdid Lyre

Buffalo skulls often served as notice boards. These messages were noticed by a traveler in 1849. Whoever wrote the second did not think much of the first. He could not spell, either.

Helpful information: an eastbound rider stops to share his knowledge of the way ahead. Pioneers asked eager questions of every traveler they met. There were quite a few people going the other way, many returning east for their families.

THE MORMONS

The Mormons were followers of a new religion, founded in 1830. They suffered from intolerance for their beliefs and eventually had to leave their homes. In 1847 they moved to remote Salt Lake, west of the Rockies.

They crossed the plains on the Platte River's north bank, to avoid hostile pioneers on the south bank. In the 1850s, other Mormons came from Europe. Many made the trek across part of the territory on foot.

The first Mormons found the valley chosen by their leader to be too dry for crops and bitterly cold in winter. They nearly starved, but in time they created a flourishing town – Salt Lake City.

Messages were left in prominent places – nailed to a tree, stuck in a cleft stick, or painted on a rock by the trail.

They warned later trains about bad water, hostile Indians, useless cutoffs, or long stretches without grass or water. If people had found good grazing or a freshwater spring some distance from the trail, they directed others there.

HELPFUL LEFTOVERS

Best bacon thrown away because it was too heavy! Cut off some and exchange it for your old bacon.

Abandoned wagons provide spare parts. Even if smashed to bits they will still be good for firewood.

Look at this Look at this! The water here is poison and we have lost six of our cattle. Do not let your cattle drink on this bottom

In 1852, Margaret Windsor, a young pioneer, took care of a baby whose mother had died.

Someone has thrown away a cast-iron stove. Just for once you can have a good baked meal.

Pioneers put up notices by the trail to warn those traveling behind of dangers. Friends who had gotten separated when trains split up or people with relatives following later left messages in the same way. One young man was in love with a girl in a train behind his, but her father disapproved. He left love letters for her on buffalo skulls, signed "Laurie," the false name they had agreed on.

Wherever the trail split, people left so many notes that the spots became known as "prairie post offices." If one route was a new "cutoff" (shortcut), messages often gave advice about taking it. It was not always good advice, because it could be based on faulty information.

At each campsite for 500 miles (800km), she had to find a mother to breast-feed it. No one refused.

An oddly marked grave is worth investigating. It may be a false one, hiding things someone means to come back for – whiskey, perhaps!

The Mormon population around Salt Lake City grew rapidly. After 1847, Mormons were running ferry services on several rivers. Many pioneers went via Salt Lake to buy flour and fresh produce.

By 1849 a civil government was set up and the Mormons applied for admission to the Union as the State of Deseret. Instead, Congress created the Territory of Utah.

Late-traveling pioneers could avoid winter dangers by staying at Salt Lake City till spring. Gold rush prospectors with no money were made to work for their keep. They often caused trouble.

Q

What sort of people would you be traveling with?
Go to pages 14-15

Should you take a cutoff just after South Pass? A mountain man selling horses by the trail says go the long way.

The cutoff saves 50 miles (80km). The oxen must go two days and a night without a drink. Weak ones will not make it.

You go the old way, past Jim Bridger's fort. You buy stores. Was that man you met sent to bring in customers?

Bridger tells you of a new cutoff to California that starts from his fort. But he wants to keep trade, so can you trust him?

Q

The thought of that wonderful land ahead keeps you going. But how will you keep in touch with your family back home?
Go to pages 40-41

THE WAYS DIVIDE
WHICH WAY WOULD YOU GO?

From Fort Laramie, the trail followed the North Platte and Sweetwater rivers up into the Rockies, crossing them at South Pass. Then the ways divided.

WAGON TRAINS could not rest long at Fort Laramie. They had to reach their journey's end before winter set in. The wagons rolled on through rough, dry, hilly country, climbing steadily into the Rockies, until in mid-July, they crossed South Pass at 8,000 feet (2,440m). Beyond the pass there was no obvious river, like the Platte, to follow. Streams ran down in folds of the Rockies, separated by mountain spurs that ran across the pioneers' way. They had to struggle over these from one river to the next.

Pioneers carve their names on Independence rock, a huge dome of granite which trains aimed to pass by the Fourth of July, Independence Day.

Children throw summer snowballs and grown-ups cheer to celebrate the crossing of South Pass. Half the journey is behind them now.

After bumping down dangerous dusty tracks in the uplands of the Rockies, the wagoners were overjoyed to discover fresh, green mountain valleys among the western slopes.

Soda Springs, on the way to Fort Hall, is a pleasant surprise. The gassy water tastes like a soda drink if you add sugar and drink it while it still fizzes. "It is fristrate [first-rate]," wrote one boy.

At Fort Hall, pioneers ask about the way ahead. They are warned it is so rough the wagons may not get through. A Californian developer urges them to turn south.

A last parting on the banks of the Snake River, where it swings north. California-bound pioneers must turn off here. There are hugs and tears as friends made on the trail have to part.

The trains wound through the western foothills of the Rockies as far as Fort Hall on the Snake River. A little beyond the fort, the pioneers bound for California turned south (if they had not already done so near Fort Bridger); the majority continued north for Oregon. People's choice was based on opinions they had heard or read. Some made up their minds only at the last minute.

All this changed dramatically when gold was discovered in California. Thousands of young men left their jobs, packed their bags, and rushed west. In 1848, only a quarter (400) of the pioneers picked California. In 1849, 25,000 went there. They jockeyed for position on the dusty trail, filled the campsites, overgrazed the grass, and shot at the Indians. Gold rushers were named "forty-niners," though the rush continued long after that year, peaking in 1852 when 50,000 went to California. The rough, impatient gold rushers were far less kind to each other than the pioneers of earlier years had been.

1849. There's gold in California! At once a huge rush begins. Wagons pour onto the trail, often twelve abreast.

Huge lines build up at rivers as wagons wait to be ferried over. Disputes over places lead to fatal shootouts.

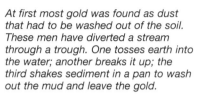

At first most gold was found as dust that had to be washed out of the soil. These men have diverted a stream through a trough. One tosses earth into the water; another breaks it up; the third shakes sediment in a pan to wash out the mud and leave the gold.

To travel fast many gold rushers take pack mules instead of wagons. Mules often do not stand the strain.

Trailside "sharks" wait for starving pioneers as they enter California, telling them that oxen are worthless there. Believing the lie, they swap them for a little flour.

AT THE MINES

As soon as you think there is gold in a particular spot, you mark it with your name, to claim your right to dig there. Someone will say he got there first. You will have to fight.

Up to your knees in mud and water all day, crouched in wind and rain, fighting to hold your own with crooks and cutthroats, it is no wonder that when you find gold you want to spend it.

You've been lucky and struck gold. You've been careful and not spent it. But the perils are not over until you get that gold back east, to the family you left.

Q

Are the Rockies the last mountains you have to cross?
Go to pages 38-39

IF YOU WERE SICK
WOULD YOU GET BETTER?

Your husband has a high fever, with vomiting and shivering fits. You beg departing wagoners to send a doctor back.

By dawn next day your husband is dead. People fear infection and will not stop. Someone throws you a spade.

You dig the grave and mark it with your husband's name. You try not to think of coyotes unearthing his body.

You decide to sell all but a single wagon and return east. The leader of an oncoming wagon train holds an auction of your husband's goods.

Q

You have got lost wandering on the plains. How can you find your train again?
Go to page 26

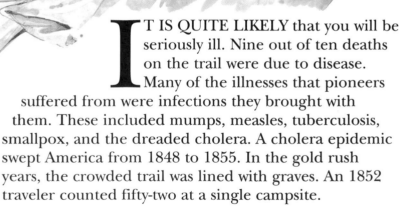

A doctor treats a cholera sufferer. Each year, a few of the pioneers would be doctors. Their help was badly needed. On horseback, a doctor could reach trains well ahead, or far behind.

Below is the true story of a day in the life of Dr. Reuben Knox, based on a letter he sent his wife in 1850. He saw up to 40 patients a day, often not getting an hour's sleep at night.

A DOCTOR'S DAY

I
T IS QUITE LIKELY that you will be seriously ill. Nine out of ten deaths on the trail were due to disease. Many of the illnesses that pioneers suffered from were infections they brought with them. These included mumps, measles, tuberculosis, smallpox, and the dreaded cholera. A cholera epidemic swept America from 1848 to 1855. In the gold rush years, the crowded trail was lined with graves. An 1852 traveler counted fifty-two at a single campsite.

3:00 A.M. Woken by a man begging me to visit someone in a camp some way off.

3:30 A.M. After riding 3 miles (5km), in fog had difficulty finding the place.

Found the patient very ill – died in half an hour. Treated three others.

Prescribed medicine. Got back 5:00 A.M. Was breakfasting when two men arrived.

5:30 A.M. The men had come from camps farther along the trail. I rode on with them.

Attended two people sick with cholera in one camp and three in another.

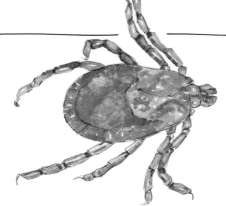

It is now known that "mountain fever" is carried by the blood-sucking Rocky Mountain wood tick (**left**). The disease damages blood vessels and causes bleeding and often death.

Let's hope you don't get a toothache on the trip, on top of all your other worries. But if you do, and can't find a doctor to pull the tooth out, a friend with some pliers might help.

HAVING TO COPE

A hospital was set up at Fort Laramie. In cholera years, it was so full that patients were treated in tents.

Some pioneers who escaped cholera believed this was due to avoiding water from the wells people had dug near the Platte River. Cholera bacteria flourish in water, so wells were a likely source of infection. You should drink running water, even if it is full of mud.

Most cholera deaths happened on the plains. Further on, the journey itself made people ill. The thin air, high in the mountains, caused headaches, nausea, and dizziness. A mysterious "mountain fever" plagued pioneers in the Rockies and beyond. On the last stretch, they got scurvy, caused by months of a diet without enough vitamin C. Sufferers grew tired and listless; their joints and gums ached; their mouths became raw, their teeth loose. They could even die. To prevent scurvy, make tea from green pine needles and drink it – a mountain man's tip few pioneers knew.

Several expectant mothers gave birth on the trail. They must have wondered if all would go well. Other women always helped, and if possible got help from a doctor.

One pioneer had his arm amputated after a rattlesnake bite. There were no anesthetics, so the person operating had to work quickly, to keep shock to a minimum. Snake bites were rare, but other accident victims might need similar treatment.

A train of eleven wagons going east in 1852 was driven by women. Their men were dead, so they were heading home.

A woman peers at sores in her child's mouth – a sign of scurvy. He needs fresh vegetables. Will the fort have any?

Cholera is a violent fever that can kill within 24 hours. It is spread by direct contact and through contaminated food and water. The cholera that swept America in waves in the nineteenth century had traveled from Asia to Europe, and from there European pioneers brought it to America.

NORTH AMERICA
EUROPE   ASIA
1848-49
1832
1873
1849
AFRICA
INDIA

Indians dreaded catching white men's diseases. So pretending you have smallpox in the camp is a good way to get rid of troublesome ones.

Galloped with another man to a wagon train. Gave medicine to his wife and child.

About 8:00 A.M., rode ahead to dying man. Only three others left alive with him.

Got back at ten, taken to train camped with 10 or 12 sick, and 6 already buried.

Stayed so long there that our company was setting off again before I returned.

All afternoon was called to camps along road. Got to our campsite six-thirty.

Two men waiting for me. I go back with one and send medicine ahead with the other.

Q

You've recovered from cholera. What other disasters might you face?
Go to pages 26-27

With winter near, speed is vital. Pack mules are fastest. You could chop up the wagon to make pack saddles.

Columbia River
Sabre River
Willamette Valley
DONNER PASS
Hastings Cutoff
Humboldt River

Oregon and California settlers said good-bye at "Farewell Bend" on Snake River. Then they went separate ways.

If you keep the wagon, throw out everything not essential. Every extra ounce wears the oxen out.

If several teams roped together cannot get a wagon up, you will have to build a winch.

Precious time is spent getting down banks and over gullies. At some precipices, animals and wagons must be lowered on ropes, one by one.

Q

Do you remember how pleasantly the journey began? Or was it just a dream?
Go to pages 18-19

THE LAST STRETCH AND THE WORST
WILL YOU MAKE IT?

THE WAY to Oregon lay across the parched plain of the Snake River. The wagons raised choking clouds of dust from its caked soil. Only dry sage plants could grow there, so the oxen became weak from hunger. Then over the steep Blue Mountains and across more dry wastes to the great Columbia River. When pioneers saw its tree-lined gorge, they were dismayed. No wagon could get through.

Pioneers spent days building rafts to float their wagons downstream. People were close to starving, and overjoyed when Indians agreed to sell them dried salmon.

The Columbia River was the biggest danger of the Oregon trip. In 1843 the Applegate family lost two boys when a boat was dashed against a rock. The boys' fathers, in another boat, were about to leap into the water, when one of the women commanded, "Men, don't leave the oars!" They too were running straight at a rock and every effort was needed to steer clear.

The Columbia River has many dangerous rapids where the boats have to be emptied. Pioneers must walk along the bank to pass the rapids. Indian porters carry the goods.

Cattle are unmanageable in small boats so have to struggle through the mountain forests that drop steeply to the river. Men from each train guide them along tracks and precipice edges.

To avoid the river perils, some 1845 pioneers tried to cross the deserts of eastern Oregon. Lost, and crazed with thirst, they decided to hang their guide. Rescuers found 20 people dead.

The pioneers headed south to reach the Humboldt River, which they followed for several weeks across a bare scorching plateau. The river gave them water and there was grass along its banks, which made the desert crossing possible. In the crowded gold rush years, it was a different matter. There was not enough grass for everyone's animals and many died of hunger.

The waters of the Humboldt River evaporate and end in a salty marsh. From this point, pioneers faced 55 miles (90km) of terrifying desert, with no water or grass. They had to rely on the small amounts they could carry. Weary and ragged, and often barely able to stagger, they got to mountain streams at last. But it was fatal to rest long. They must cross the Sierra Nevada by October.

TO CALIFORNIA

If coyotes find you alone and weak they will surround you, day and night. They eat dead bodies.

Where the Humboldt River ends, cut marsh grass for your animals to eat in the desert.

Beyond the sands you see the mountains rising, but you will never reach them if your water runs out.

You might get help from one of the relief teams that Californians sent with food and water to meet incoming pioneers.

Trapped in the Sierras in 1846, members of the Donner party make a desparate bid to cross a snow-blocked pass (now called the Donner Pass), to get help for the rest. Of the seventeen who set out, seven reached the California valley. To survive, they had eaten the bodies of dead companions.

Q

Women took over if their men were sick or died. They drove wagons and rounded up the animals. But was that their normal role? *Go to pages 22-23*

THE DONNER STORY

Jacob and George Donner's party overloaded and started late. At Fort Bridger they took an untried cutoff and spent weeks in boulder-strewn canyons. Then they rested too long.

In late October, they began to climb the Sierras. Within a week, the 87 people were snowbound. Food ran out. People ate fur rugs and glue made from bones.

Californian rescuers could not cross until February. When they reached the survivors they found some half mad, They, too, had lived by eating frozen companions. Only 47 survived.

A NEW HOME
HOW WOULD YOU START?

Oregon winters are warmer than back east. You can sow a winter wheat crop as well as a spring one.

Grass grows well throughout the year, so the cattle can graze outside all winter. There is no need to make hay.

The Oregon forests are full of game. Salmon is plentiful, and you can fish for trout all year long.

Fruit trees do well, if you can get plants. A man came west with a wagonload of 700 young trees. By propagating them, he made a fortune.

Q
What hairbreadth escapes will you describe when you reminisce about the trail?
Go to pages 36-37

The vegetable patch is behind the cabin, out of the reach of straying poultry and animals.

The cabin is put up quickly as a temporary home. It is a single room, with sleeping space for the children in the loft. Behind it is a barn, with room for the cattle.

Later, when you build a larger house, the old log cabin will make a useful shed. In the meantime, it is much cozier than the wagon.

Stone footings raise the cabin off the ground so the damp soil won't rot the timbers.

AT THE END OF THE TRAIL, what relief the travelers felt! Even those who had made the journey without disasters (and many did) were worn down by its hardship and uncertainty. Fears, doubts – was it all a wild goose chase? – and homesickness had dogged them on the way. "I feel tired and weary, O, the luxury of a house, a house!" an unhappy traveler wrote longingly. Now at last that dream could come true.

The first task was to stake a claim to land. A bill before Congress in 1841 had proposed that each Oregon settler be allowed 640 free acres (259ha), plus 160 (65ha) more for a wife and for each child. People felt this was the go-ahead for them to help themselves, even before Oregon officially became part of the United States in 1859.

CABIN BUILDING
Your first task is to build a cabin – a temporary home.

Find a level patch, not too far from water, and clear the undergrowth.

Cut down trees that will provide the longest logs, as log length dictates cabin size.

You need oxen to haul the logs Others may lend oxen if you do not have enough.

Cut a curved notch near the ends of each log. The notches will hold logs in place.

Neighbors often share the work to put up a house. Here, they drop a log into position.

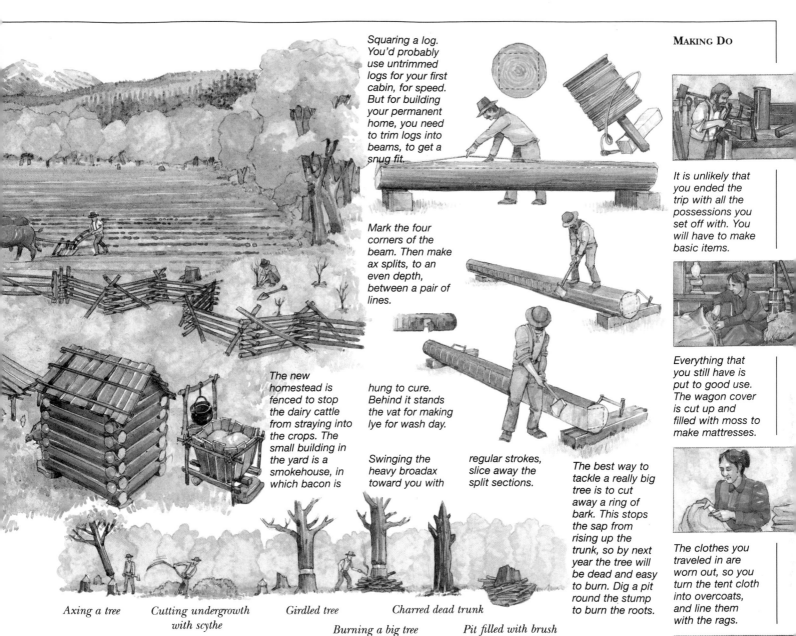

Squaring a log. You'd probably use untrimmed logs for your first cabin, for speed. But for building your permanent home, you need to trim logs into beams, to get a snug fit.

Mark the four corners of the beam. Then make ax splits, to an even depth, between a pair of lines.

The new homestead is fenced to stop the dairy cattle from straying into the crops. The small building in the yard is a smokehouse, in which bacon is hung to cure. Behind it stands the vat for making lye for wash day.

Swinging the heavy broadax toward you with regular strokes, slice away the split sections.

The best way to tackle a really big tree is to cut away a ring of bark. This stops the sap from rising up the trunk, so by next year the tree will be dead and easy to burn. Dig a pit round the stump to burn the roots.

Axing a tree   *Cutting undergrowth with scythe*   *Girdled tree*   *Charred dead trunk*

Burning a big tree   *Pit filled with brush*

It is unlikely that you ended the trip with all the possessions you set off with. You will have to make basic items.

Everything that you still have is put to good use. The wagon cover is cut up and filled with moss to make mattresses.

The clothes you traveled in are worn out, so you turn the tent cloth into overcoats, and line them with the rags.

That buffalo hide you bought from Indians on the plains has come in very useful. You nail it up as a draft excluder over the door.

Most settlers turned south, into the valley of the Willamette River. There was already a village (grandly named Oregon City) on its banks. It had been settled in 1842 by the director of the Hudson's Bay Company's headquarters at nearby Fort Vancouver. A scattering of retired Company trappers and American sea traders were already farming in the valley. As the pioneers fanned out over the valley they must have been cheered by the flourishing autumn grass and magnificent trees with tall, thick trunks. They could borrow tools and seed from the fort and pay the loan back with next year's profits. Families sharing labor could have a cabin built, fields fenced, and a crop sown by the following spring.

As the walls get high the logs are hauled into place on sloping timbers, called skids.

The end walls are built into gables, the roof ridgepole is put across and rafters added.

The chimney should be stone or brick, but you could use wood lined with clay.

Cut out the door, windows, and fireplace after the walls and roof are complete.

To make the cabin weather-proof, fill chinks with mud or clay and pebbles.

The roof is wooden shingles, made by splitting short lengths of timber into slices.

Q

Did you remember to bring carpentry tools?

Go to pages 16-17

By the 1850s, wagon trains, often nose to tail might have to travel late into the night to find a vacant campsite.

Litter lined the route – objects from overloaded wagons, broken wheels, bones and carcasses of animals.

Indians got no sympathy from impatient gold rushers, some of whom boasted of shooting every Indian they saw.

White "Indians" appeared in the 1850s. Bandits in Indian dress, with darkened skin, ambushed wagons and let Indians get the blame.

LIFE IN THE WEST
WHAT HAPPENED NEXT?

A QUARTER OF A MILLION people went west between 1840 and 1860; their wagons wore ruts so deep that some can still be seen. New farms and cities proved that North America was not too wide for one nation to fill. In 1846, Britain agreed that Oregon belonged to the U.S.; in 1847, Mexico yielded California.

The losers in this story are the Indians. They did not understand the white people's attitude to land. Instead of using what it had to offer, white men wanted to alter it, build on it, fence it, and own it. They came in unbelievable numbers to do this. Then the Indians saw that their homelands would be taken from them and realized they were not powerful enough to resist.

This picture is based on an 1862 photo of Plains Indians by a new house. Some are dressed like whites. "What has happened to our life?" their faces seem to ask.

U.S. government officials meet Plains Indian chiefs at Medicine Lodge Creek, Kansas, in 1867, to ask them to go to reservations and allow roads and railroads to be built across their lands.

Pony Express rider with California–Missouri mail. He changes horses every 10–15 miles (16–24km). A new rider takes over every 75 miles (120km). The fastest time was 7 days 17 hours. The express lasted only from 1860 to 1861, when the transcontinental telegraph put it out of business.

Q Had the Indians always been unfriendly?
Go to pages 24-25

Military outposts, like Fort Kearney, made pioneers feel safe. The Indians were not reassured. They grew more obstructive, and heavy-handed army reactions made confrontation worse.

The whites introduced diseases, took Indian lands, killed buffalo, and fenced hunting grounds. In the Indian Wars from the 1860s, to the 1880s both whites and Indians were massacred.

A tribe leaves its homeland to move to a reservation, an area chosen by the U.S. government, out of the settlers' way. Many tribes agreed to do this, rather than fight.

California and Oregon were linked by stagecoach in the 1850s, but an east–west service took much more organization. A route had to be chosen (which caused lots of argument) and relay stations for changes of horses set up along the way.

From the 1850s, the trail was transformed. Surveyors mapped it; roads were built and rivers bridged.

The distance separating East from West was the next problem to be overcome. By the 1860s, stagecoaches traveled from the Missouri to the Pacific in twenty days. Riders of the Pony Express took half that. The transcontinental telegraph, completed in October 1861, sent instant messages. By 1869 a railroad spanned the country. Pioneers no longer had to drive.

Passengers on the plains seize a chance for "sport." The herds that the Plains Indians depended on were dwindling fast. There had been 75 million buffalo on the plains. By 1900, about a thousand were left.

Trailside traders set up shacks selling animals, drink, supplies – anything pioneers might run out of.

Towns sprang up almost overnight, wherever businessmen thought the new railroad was likely to make a stop.

Better plows that cut tough prairie turf made farming the "American desert" possible at last. In the 1880s, the wild prairie began to vanish.

SPANNING THE COUNTRY

In 1865 two rail companies started building toward each other from each coast, to bridge the gap. Getting enough workmen was a major problem. Chinese were hired at the Pacific end.

The railroad builders had to span ravines, tunnel mountains, and keep food reaching the tracklayers. Sometimes workers had to fight Indians desperate to stop the "iron horse."

May 10, 1869. The two lines meet just north of the Great Salt Lake. The railroad companies' presidents finish the work by driving in a ceremonial "last spike," made of gold.

Q
Where was the "American desert"?
Go to page 9

THE PIONEERS have told their own story. The journey was such a spectacular event in their lives that it prompted many men and women who would never have thought of themselves as writers to describe it. On the trail they sent letters and kept diaries. Reminiscences were later published. By the 1870s the earliest pioneers were coming to a time of life when memories are precious. They formed societies – the Oregon Pioneer Association, the Society of California Pioneers – to keep old companions in touch and to gather material about the trail. Nearly 800 documents of trail experiences have been preserved.

Artist George Catlin painting a Mandan chief in 1832. (**Left**). The finished portrait. Catlin was fascinated by the Plains Indians. He studied many tribes and pleaded for their way of life to be preserved.

Narcissa Whitman

Marcus Whitman

In 1836 Narcissa Whitman accompanied her husband, Dr. Marcus Whitman, to bring Christianity to the Indians of the Far West. The Whitmans were killed in 1847.

Francis Parkman's book, The Oregon Trail, *became an American classic. It describes a tour he made in 1846 over the plains. He and a cousin set off with a guide and baggage team to study Indian life and had many amazing experiences.*

Parkman did not cross the Rockies. He was not a pioneer but a young man fresh from college, seeking adventure.

Sketch from an 1849 diary shows a gold rusher staggering into California, his mules dead, his food finished, his baggage lost, still with a long way to go.

Guidebooks for would-be pioneers began to appear in the gold rush years, giving advice and often rather sketchy route information. Joseph E. Ware's guidebook was warmly recommended in newspapers of 1849.

When someone left behind back East got a letter at last, it was eagerly read and often lovingly kept. New arrivals sent advice to relatives about to follow the trail.

The Sioux chieftain Little Crow being photographed in 1858. At that time photographs involved sitting still in a studio.

1850 gold prospector Byron McKinstry records how a companion said "My God, McKinstry, why do you write about this trip so you can remember it? All I hope is to get home alive as soon as possible so I can forget."

Later settlers stop to pose for a photograph, which survives. Photography was so new in the 1840s there are no photos of the first pioneers, but these faces show the toughness and determination that got them there.

Diaries and letters let us experience the journey with all the vividness of being there and not knowing what the next day may bring. Government documents, newspaper articles, letters to the press, pioneer society pamphlets – these enable historians to fill in the background. But there is something else we want to know. What did the unspoiled West actually look like? Luckily, just as the Plains Indians' way of life was about to be destroyed, it was painstakingly recorded by artists of the 1830s. The breathtaking magnificence of the scenery, as the pioneers saw it, is captured in the landscapes of Albert Bierstadt, who went west with a government survey in 1858.

TIMESPAN

1778 British explorer Captain James Cook sails up the Pacific coast of North America and enters Nootka Sound (just north of modern Oregon). He claims the area for Britain. His men obtain furs that, on their way home, they sell in China at vast profit.

1780s The English establish trading posts on Nootka Sound to obtain furs in the region, which comes to be known as "Oregon country." (A vast area, it included the present states of Oregon, Washington, Wyoming, and British Columbia.)

1792 American Robert Gray, trading for furs along the north Pacific coast, in his ship the *Columbia*, discovers a huge river, which he names after his ship. He claims the area for the United States.

1803 The United States government purchases the North American territory known as Louisiana from the French.

1804 U.S. President Thomas Jefferson sends an expedition, led by Meriwether Lewis and William Clark, to explore the new territory in the hope of finding an overland route to fur-rich Oregon country.

1806 Lewis and Clark find no easy route but return with accounts of the wealth of furs obtainable in the Rockies.

1807 John Colter, who had been on Lewis and Clark's expedition, and Manuel Lisa open up the fur trade in the Rockies.

1811 New York merchant John Jacob Astor, owner of the American Fur Company trading near the Great Lakes, tries to break into the Oregon trade. He founds a fur-trading post on the Columbia River but the project runs into disaster and fails.

1818 An Anglo-American agreement states that the Oregon region shall be jointly occupied by both nations. The British pay little heed to it.

1821 Mexico gains independence from Spain. American traders begin taking wagonloads of goods along the trail to the New Mexico capital, Santa Fe.

1821 British fur companies competing in Canada are merged to form the Hudson's Bay Company, which dominates the Oregon fur trade. It builds Fort Vancouver on the Columbia River.

1822 William Ashley and Andrew Henry found the Rocky Mountain Fur Company (later taken over by the American Fur Company) and organize a system of buying furs from trappers (mountain men) under contract to them.

1824 Mountain man Jed Smith discovers South Pass, Wyoming.

1826 Smith pioneers an overland route to California.

1830–1840 American merchants living in Mexican-owned California encourage the idea of American settlement.

1831 Pioneer enthusiast Hall Jackson Kelly organizes a pioneer society to promote Oregon.

1831 Four Indians from west of the Rockies travel with some fur traders to St Louis.

1832 In an attempt to start a colony, Kelly sets off for Oregon with a handful of followers. He gets there two years later, via New Orleans, Mexico City, and California, having lost all his companions on the way. His attempt is a failure, and he returns home by ship in 1835.

1832 Spring Businessman Nathaniel Wyeth forms a company to set up businesses in Oregon. He sends a supply ship round Cape Horn to the Pacific to meet him. He and twenty-four companions then set off west, with mules loaded with supplies to sell to mountain men on the way.

1832 October Wyeth and some of his companions, guided for stretches by various fur traders, reach Fort Vancouver. They are the first party of westbound Americans to use what was later called the Oregon Trail.

1832 Wyeth's supply ship is lost at sea and his venture fails. He returns east but three of his companions remain and become the first American settlers in Oregon.

1833 Mountain man Joseph Walker finds a safer trail to California along the Humboldt River.

1834 The Methodist Board of Missions sends church minister Jason Lee to Oregon to convert its so-called Flathead Indians. He visits the Willamette Valley area and becomes convinced that its climate, soil, and trade links with California and China make it the ideal spot for an American colony.

1836 Dr. Marcus Whitman, his wife Narcissa, and another missionary couple reach Oregon. These women are the first to travel the Oregon Trail. Up to now, pack mules or horses have been used on the trail. Marcus Whitman struggles to bring a wagon through but is forced to abandon it in difficult country west of the Rockies.

1840 American Joel Walker travels to Oregon, in the company of three missionaries. As he is not a missionary or a trader but is going solely to make a home there, he is considered to be the first overland pioneer.

1841 Sixty-nine pioneers go west to California or Oregon.

1841 Dr. Elijah White, newly returned from a sea trip to Oregon, speaks at meetings and vigorously promotes emigration.

1842 Dr. White leads a party of 18 wagons to Oregon.

1843 Almost 1,000 pioneers go West, the first large migration and the first to get wagons through to Oregon.

1846 Britain acknowledges U.S. ownership of Oregon up to the 49th parallel.

1846 War between the United States and Mexico.

1847 Mexico is defeated and in 1848 signs a treaty surrendering California to the United States.

1848 Gold is discovered in the American River, California. The news travels by ship around Cape Horn and reaches the East Coast by autumn.

1849 The gold rush begins. Enormous numbers of people set out for California as soon as the weather permits.

1850 California becomes the thirty-first state of the Union.

1852 Peak emigration year: 50,000 go to California and 10,000 to Oregon.

1858 The first stagecoach service linking East and West begins to operate.

1859 Oregon is admitted to the Union as the thirty-third state.

1860 April to 1861 October The Pony Express carries mail from St. Joseph, Missouri, to Sacramento, California.

October 1861 The transcontinental telegraph line is completed.

1869 Completion of the coast-to-coast railroad ends transcontinental wagon travel.

HAVE YOU SURVIVED?

Q 1 If you were on the lookout for the "cow column" you would be expecting to find:

A a list of cattle prices in the Independence newspaper?
B a desert stretch lined with the carcasses of pioneers' cattle?
C a slow-moving wagon train with large herds of cattle?

Q 2 Your family did not travel up the Platte River by boat. Was this because:

A it would not take them in the right direction?
B it was too shallow?
C it had dangerous rapids and waterfalls?

Q 3 Buffalo are approaching the camp at speed. Should you:

A do nothing, knowing that buffalo are not aggressive?
B set fire to the grass?
C pack up, hitch your oxen to the wagons, and try to get everything out of the way?

Q 4 Was the American Fur Company trading post at:

A Fort Laramie?
B Fort Bridger?
C Fort Hall?

Q 5 As a precaution against getting cholera should you:

A avoid water that has been used by other people?
B avoid getting ticks in the mountains?
C avoid a diet that lacks vitamin C?

Q 6 Would you find a "prairie post office" at:

A Independence?
B Fort Laramie?
C several places along the trail?

Q 7 Is a cut-off:

A an ambush?
B an alternative route?
C a sawed-off shotgun?

Q 8 Is a gold digger called a "forty-niner" because:

A gold was found at latitude 49?
B the gold rush began in 1849?
C miners over fifty lied about their age?

Q 9 Who took over Fort Laramie in 1849?

A the Sioux Indians?
B the U.S. Army?
C the British government?

Q 10 Are buffalo chips:

A buffalo dung used to make a fire?
B buffalo-skin trousers?
C potatoes fried in buffalo fat?

Q 11 Was a mountain man:

A a U.S. soldier serving in the Rockies?
B an Indian of the High Plains?
C a fur trapper who lived in the wilderness?

Q 12 Would South Pass have led you:

A over the Blue Mountains?
B over the Rockies?
C over the Sierra Nevada?

Q 13 Was a bull boat:

A a cattle ferry?
B a Missouri steamboat chartered by pioneers?
C a round, hide-covered boat?

Q 14 Are shingles:

A flat loaves baked in a covered frying pan?
B slivers of wood used to roof houses?
C chains for hitching oxen to a wagon?

Q 15 A walking larder was:

A a person who had overeaten and could not ride?
B a portable meat cupboard?
C animals you took along for food?

Q 16 A prairie dog is:

A a plains rodent that lives in a burrow?
B a wolfish type of dog kept by the plains Indians?
C a sausage made of buffalo meat?

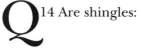

Count up your correct answers and discover your survival rating on page 48.

GLOSSARY

ALKALINE containing alkali, a chemical substance.

ANESTHETICS painkilling substances.

AXLE strong wooden crosspiece connecting opposite wheels.

BOWIE KNIFE broad-bladed knife for cutting and chopping, said to have been designed by early nineteenth-century frontiersman Jim Bowie.

COYOTES scavenging animals of the dog family.

DRAFT ANIMALS animals used to pull vehicles.

DYSENTERY an inflammation of the intestines causing painful diarrhea.

FLATBOAT rectangular boat made of straight planks.

FORD a point where a river is shallow enough for people to wade or ride across it.

GROUNDWATER water that collects naturally some distance below ground level.

GULLY a steep-sided channel through which a stream runs.

HARDWOOD durable wood, not soft timber like pine.

INAUGURAL ADDRESS the first speech made by a new U.S. president.

JACK a portable machine for raising heavy objects from below. To use a jack.

LYE homemade detergent made by soaking wood ashes.

MOCCASIN a heelless shoe, originally made from buffalo hide.

PALISADED defended by a palisade, a fence of close-set stakes.

PIONEERS the first people to settle in a territory.

PLAINS INDIANS Indians of the plains east of the Rockies. Most depended on the buffalo for survival.

PRICKLY PEAR a spiny cactus.

RABIES a fatal disease of warm-blooded animals and humans, affecting the nervous system. An infected animal transmits the disease by biting another animal or person.

SAGE PLANT a low, gray shrub unrelated to the herb used in stuffing.

SNAG a tree that has been swept into a river and remains, semisubmerged, with its roots in the riverbed and its branches held at a dangerous angle by the current.

SQUAW an Indian woman.

TELEGRAPH a system of sending messages in the form of pulses of electric current traveling along wires. The pulses are decoded and turned into a written message by a receiving machine.

TEPEE a tent of buffalo hide, lived in by Plains Indians.

WINCH an apparatus for hauling heavy objects, by means of a rope wound up around a crosspiece that was rotated by a handle.

INDEX

ANSWERS
HAVE YOU SURVIVED?

Here are the answers, with pages to turn to if you need an explanation. Count up your correct answers and find out your survival rating.

1 (C) – see page 19
2 (B) – see page 20
3 (B) – see page 21
4 (A) – see page 28
5 (A) – see page 35
6 (C) – see page 31
7 (B) – see page 31
8 (B) – see page 33

9 (B) – see page 29
10 (A) – see page 23
11 (C) – see page 6
12 (B) – see page 32
13 (C) – see page 26
14 (B) – see page 39
15 (C) – see page 16
16 (A) – see page 21

16 Excellent! Good luck in your new home.
13 – 15 You're there, but you've lost a few things on the way.
9 – 12 You have been taking it too easy. Remember that you need your wits about you on the trail.
4 – 8 You will be lucky if you get there before winter.
0 – 3 Disastrous! You are one of the unfortunate ones who never reached their journey's end.

ACKNOWLEDGEMENTS
The Salariya Book Co Ltd would like to thank the following people for their assistance:
Sarah Ridley
Eileen Batterberry

PRINTED IN BELGIUM BY
proost
INTERNATIONAL BOOK PRODUCTION